COMFORTING THE WILDERNESS

The Wesleyan Poetry Program : Volume 87

COMFORTING
THE WILDERNESS

Poems

ROBERT B. SHAW

Wesleyan University Press
Middletown, Connecticut

Sixteen of these poems first appeared in *Poetry*. Others have been published in the following English and American magazines: *Isis, Carcanet, Poetry/Nation, The Harvard Advocate, Poetry Miscellany,* and *Sequoia.* In addition, some have appeared in two small booklets published in England: *In Witness* (Anvil Press Poetry, London, 1972), and *Curious Questions* (Carcanet Press, Oxford, 1970). Six poems were anthologized in *Ten American Poets* (ed. James Atlas, Carcanet Press, 1973).

The publisher gratefully acknowledges the support of the publication of this book by the Andrew W. Mellon Foundation.

Designed by Susan Kelsey

Library of Congress Cataloging in Publication Data

Shaw, Robert Burns, 1947–
    Comforting the wilderness.

    (Wesleyan poetry program)
    I. Title.
PR 6069.H394C6   811'.5'4   77-74603
ISBN 0-8195-2087-X
ISBN 0-8195-1087-4 pbk.

Manufactured in the United States of America
First edition

To Robert Fitzgerald

ἔχω γὰρ ἄχω διὰ σὲ κοὐκ ἄλλον βροτῶν

CONTENTS

I

Boston Sunday Dinner   11

3 A.M., January 1   13

Janus   14

Tagalong   16

Gargoyle   17

Jack-O'-Lantern   18

A Study   19

Antecedents   20

From Ashes   22

Getting On   24

Roethke   25

Watching the Street   27

A Book of Ikons   28

An Old Route   30

In the Attic   32

Snake Crossing   34

A Man and His Watch   35

II

Burning Abortive Poems   37

The Taste of Failure   39

Skimming a Surface   40

Aesop in Our Time   41

A Letter from Behind the Lines   42

Not Answering Letters   43

To James Atlas   44

The First Day of Spring 46

Mid-July 47

Small Hours 48

Morning Message 50

Renovations 51

Looking Out 53

Simile 54

III

Safe on Friendly Soil 55

IV

Birth of a Critical Spirit 59

The Poem 61

A Living 62

In Witness 63

Recessional 65

There 67

The Pause 68

Heat Wave 69

Climb and Cloudburst 70

Practice 72

Grass Widows 73

On Becoming an Altar Boy 74

Museum Coins 75

Old Photograph 77

Another Day 79

COMFORTING THE WILDERNESS

I

BOSTON SUNDAY DINNER

More grandly than a camel kneeling down
in desert twilight she assumed her place,
motioning me to join her at her right.
Spooky, I thought, this dining in state for two,
at one corner of a table built for twelve.
Her hand lay on the table like pressed wax,
the bones too easily seen, but beautiful.
A prism hung to the cord of a window blind
sprinkled a bracelet of rainbow on her wrist.
December; and the light was dropping off early,
but even in winter dusk her silver showed
the chastened glow of a century's polishing.
I puzzled over the function of my forks,
abashed by the graying, apron-clad retainer
shuffling toward me with a plate of soup.
The last remaining help, unused to company.
Most of the talk has left me. Only a few
sentences I remember, each one prefaced
by an apologetic almost-cough.
"Literary men now are no longer what
they were in my day, in my father's day.
My father used to see James Russell Lowell
walking on Brattle Street in his English suits.
You know that he was our Ambassador.
I don't suppose we've had a poet since
presentable enough for such an office.
Well, poets may be better unpresentable...."
I mused over the room we just had left
and would return to: utterly insufficient
fireplace, sooty portraits, sets of Scott
and Trollope, obvious volumes read to pieces.
Fur of her three cats tufted the furniture....

I made my answers while the rainbow band
retreated down the table from us, flashed
at last on the far paneling; when I looked
again, was gone entirely. Shadow filled
the air like a fine ash; suddenly even she
began to feel it. So she called out, "Emily!
"If you please! The lights!" (No guest of hers
rose from her table to approach a light switch.)
Again the gray lady entered, touched the wall,
illumining us, and turned to take our dishes.
I saw their faces side by side for an instant
under the good light. Sisters they might have been.

As if a talking desert got up and went . . .
The party's moved. Over an hour ago now.

Those veteran guests decamped happily enough,
facing the year to come stunned only mildly.

Now the street darkens, the mercury dutifully
drops, the steam bangs up and around in the pipes.

Now as I've noticed before, when you and I
are alone, work is what saves us. Minor chores!—

put your house in order, put your troubles to bed,
try not to be or see yourself or think . . .

You have been emptying out more ashtrays
than I could fill myself in my life;

I have been gathering up more glasses
than I could bear to break now for effect.

An ache kneels in the right side of my head
and won't move on out. I seem now to see our

years as a pack of scenes narrowly avoided,
fronts for our friends who might offer suggestions.

But outside it's colder than ever. In this town,
in winter, in need, justice is oddly even:

Bums have found heat by this time of night
by slumming in bus stations. They have

a place to go, we have a place to stay.

JANUS

Wise tribe, the old Romans—
spiriting up an adequate
god to attend to every angle,
packing the Pantheon.
Take this old retainer, erected
where you would nowadays expect
a ticket booth or a hatrack:
patron alike of low posterns
and of exalted portals,
god of gateways, steady-lipped
genius of entrance and egress.

Pre-dating Peter
as keeper of the keys,
he carries a commanding bunch
in his left hand, a hefty staff
warningly in his right.
For a deity whose proper
feast falls on New Year's
he appears awfully sober,
even a trifle dull,
except for those alarming double
features from the neck up.

Consider how he stood
at the City gate, one set
of eyes stiff on the lookout
for the foretold invader,
the other pair detailed to cover
possible subversives.
Or in the temple porch, he
marked a man's going out
even as his coming in.
Men slept easier
for this unfaltering vigilance—
odd as that may seem to us

who wince at supervision.
If he sees whatever passes,
that is reason ample enough
to kindle me to mistrust.
I wouldn't want, or stand to have him
darkening my own doorway—
tough-whiskered as Saturn,
cut from the same gray stone,
flinty-eared as midwinter,
two-faced as time.

TAGALONG

That idiot face keeps following you around,
bouncing, bobbling just behind
one or another shoulder, like a balloon
hitched to the back of your belt.
Always you swing around to find it smiling,
the silliest full moon of a face,
coming along for the ride.

And if you ever surprise it with
a whistling fist to the cheek,
it will neither explode nor shrink in pain.
The harder you hit it the harder
it smiles, bruising to the most beautiful colors:
violet patches, coppery green at the edges.

Nothing, you discover, can ever pull down
the corners of that mouth:
it smiles and goes on smiling
because there is nothing behind it.
You smile a good deal less nowadays yourself
because of what is behind you.
That face.

GARGOYLE

An ornamental bung,
a dragon-dog in little,
a throat without a tongue
to sample its own spittle:

whatever I may be,
harpy or horned toad,
is all the same to me.
I labor to erode.

Good Christians, as you go
about your wonted kneeling,
be thankful you're below
a serviceable ceiling.

For centuries I've craned
my neck above your city
and never yet complained.
I am above your pity.

And you are under mine.
I dream: a day will come
of which I am the sign.
Smitten grotesquely dumb,

you'll glare to see each other sprout
tusk, antler, serrate tail,
and the appalling snout.
I trust fate not to fail,

when even today on just
and unjust Heaven can strew
that soot-laden rain I must
catch, convey and spew.

JACK-O'-LANTERN

Candle, spoon and carving knife:
nearing the vigil of the dead,
let's impose a little life
upon a ripening, faceless head.

Slice and pry the handled top,
shovel out the mush and seeds,
cut—before we hear the clop,
coming too close, of chalky steeds.

Two triangles make the eyes,
another makes a classic nose;
three teeth, square and oversize,
complete a countenance that glows

all night by its captive wick,
its parody of intellect.
Idle amusement for the quick.
And yet the venturous dead are checked:

shades of traitors that are given
one night's leave of Satan's jaws;
throngs of warlocks; wild unshriven
things with lammergeyer claws;

bogies by the wide heavens abhorred
witness their own defective will
when they flee this grinning gourd
presiding on our window sill.

Of whom or what an effigy,
that is for itself to know
until All Hallows' turn us free
to lift the cranial lid and blow.

A STUDY

Hung to the ceiling's centerpoint, he seems
to accent every other vertical.
This is the way a room grows tall in dreams,
escaping up beyond human recall.
Too much is here to take in at once, and we
hunt with our eyes for something familiar to hold to.
Twilight eddies in corners, almost blue.
Afternoon dust alights on the motionless globe.
There where he laid it aside the study key
glints at a grazing touch of departing sun.
Here the feeling is one of work routinely done,
of wastebaskets put to use with a seemly frequency.
Docketed, paid bills, uncluttered blotters testify
to an archaic, resolute but affable efficiency.

That was it: having made his effects as neat
as might befit a man of considered action,
he set himself to perform this final feat
of incredible abstraction.
Drawn by his weight the ceiling creaks.
Hairline cracks begin to radiate
outward from the firm hook that held the chandelier.
Discouraging inquiry, he sets the dominant line
toward any who would seek for entrance here.
For see, around his axis gravitate
such bevies of objects now bereft of care:
pipe racks and pens and the heads of state, signed,
serve only to frame a dangled figure and await
the paced evaporation of his tension.
And we, his audience, who forced the door
open to see him, see him in just this state
and gather to a quiet minute's halt here before
a willing suspension.

ANTECEDENTS

I knew a man who was born the day Yeats died.
He said the same hour. He implied other things.
     I find that less auspicious beginnings
     manage to preoccupy me more:

those of true originals without any recourse
to metempsychosis to explain away
     that deep-abiding incongruity
     goading them young from their homes.

Johnson could never have stayed for long in Lichfield:
stalking the Strand with the irascible dignity
     of a great, offended tom turkey,
     "mad all his life, at least not sober,"

he had arrived where he could practice survival.
Neither could Thetford village where Tom Paine was
     apprenticed to make corset stays
     retain his prickly allegiance.

It even must have been difficult being Nietzsche,
brought up by maiden aunts. You look for hints
     and auguries, you find maiden aunts
     and orphans in drab circumstances.

But nothing so tangible as frayed rugs and fractured
crockery persuaded them to seek a release;
     a phantom pain, such as amputees
     feel, drew them from their cradles of intellect.

Estranged so early, those singular children
with more on their minds than the aunts ever could guess
     must have prized moments of idleness
     which they could pass standing by windows,

losing themselves in simply watching the dust
passing wagons were lifting up on the highroad.
     Often they were accounted sad
     and willful in such reveries.

And rightly so: tense, pale, determined,
every game they played said, Don't tread on me.
  There was nothing to do but to be
  distastefully stern or unreasonably patient,

suffering their unkind, their thankless scrutiny
till the day came when they were done being noticed
  for oddness, done having their meanings missed,
  done having the dust of those houses

rising behind them unseen as they paced the floors.
The day came when they shook that dust from their hair
  and went questing a change of air
  and habit, invading the heedless city,

there to be reborn in the fitful current
of years and of callings. And their native places
  soon grew depressed, showed traces
  of age, lost all thought of the lost sons.

FROM ASHES

Sometimes a man comes home to find his house
burnt to the floor and no fire left to fight.
Stray sparks glint between splinters of glass.
No one is home and no home stands and it is a cold night.

And the scene is deep in trees. And no moon shows.
Trees never caught and they keep him there in the dark.
Pine trees sifting the wind bend and brush elbows,
differing whether he'll bother setting to work

to set to rights the black hulks of his beams
leaning unevenly over his late concerns—
the ashy pulp of papers and books whose names
are hard now to remember. Now he learns

to notice the basic, charred bones of the house,
bent pipes, fused wires, a battered sink—
boring necessities made precious by loss.
Hearing the gossipy pines, he tries to think:

Was it lightning? Did the cat chew on a wire?
Did the wind help? Why didn't he live in town,
where neighbors are near and trees are tame and fire
attracts attention? Nobody's house burns down

nowadays. All his woes are out of style,
like his address. Who else happens to be
deprived of a big red hook-and-ladder while
flames eat up his shingles? He can see

only so far: Privacy didn't pay.
His one pet lies minus her nine lives.
Now what? Walk off and leave it, the way
men will abandon bad cars or their wives?

O ashes will all be cold by morning, morning,
mutter the pines, his proxy family, till he
turns on his heel, hard. But he hears a ping
down by his foot: this is that extra key,

scuffed from under what was a doormat. When
he holds it in his hand his trees become
silent, as if suddenly seared. A man
clings to his title. Sometimes a man comes home.

GETTING ON

Deep in every autumn day,
in the same out-of-doors,
we practice in an antique play—
bending among resident flowers
that are bored at being ours,
knowing every line we have to say.

In back of us, your father's house
spills an advancing shadow;
now before it touches us
we could make our move and go
where our tiredness tells us to,
away from every autumn garden pose.

But we hear that we are bound
by a human pride of place
even to minor plots of ground,
defending them with inner praise
even as seasons and our days
rise and are meanly downed.

Sunset and dying swan
figure in older-fashioned dreams;
but the light above the lawn,
retreating, folds away its beams
all too busily. So, it seems
easy enough to see how things are done.

Air that floats above your head
is the air brightness fell from;
both of us are fitly bred
as a bright chrysanthemum
caught between your finger and your thumb.
Old words can wait till they are said.

ROETHKE

Grief, what a long way
you had to travel:

coming to me
from the far coast,
risen from the western sea,

moving in over me
like a change in weather,
clouding over all the teeming
map of his discovery.

I remember reading:
in dreams he drove
down country turnpikes,
interminable by dark.
No signs anywhere, no place to park.
Woods ran alongside.

It seems every word
he wrote now must take
its chances, taking root
or not in the gray earth.
Maybe a good many
will grow now, and sigh
beyond captivity,
comforting the wilderness.

I don't know where
you might find him now.
I hope: There,

where the rain has found
a father, where the ground
calls out to a new coming,
where the snows are over
and done, and where
(simply as a matter

of habit) every clover
is four-leaved
for luck

as I hope in the end he believed.

But how many ways
there are of being lost.
Sometimes I think he found them all.

WATCHING THE STREET

Where is tomorrow's lover
beguiling time today?
Under what lucky cover
do those desired limbs play

lazily, and with whom, while we
curse each hour's constraint,
bashing away at destiny
with unabashed complaint?

Crammed traffic, dubious dealing
till dusk drum on below;
now the white moths come wheeling
round a cold, pillared glow.

While charms we'd cultivated
tatter to fruitless seed,
too fixedly instated
even to sleep or feed,

we sit here, undemanded,
wed to the window sill,
worn-eyed and idle-handed,
manning a vigil still

for the one shape our discerning
will lift from the swaggering mass . . .
But why is the window turning
into a looking glass?

A BOOK OF IKONS

Saints enjoy, for certain items,
more of a memory than we do.
They are said not to forget us
when we fall to forgetting ourselves.

I have been devoting study
lately to a collection of them.
Some are draped in scarlet,
some are wrought all of gold,

any that are men are bearded
and are typically bald, befitting
latter-day Elishas.
Some are seen handling swords

or feather pens, incurious whether
one might be mightier.
One man carries a key.
Some are shown with open books

in their pale, unknuckled fingers
that appear not to have to grip.
Some, it is true, have been
honored with their wounds, but

that naive bleeding cannot
siphon the composure from their hands.
They are waiting patiently
to leave behind their relics.

Concerning their women: they
are hooded, hard-sorrowing, and
are unassailable forever.
Women like that we no longer have with us.

After an hour of viewing, their
eyes could all be one eye,
tender as a drop of tar
widening in the sun,

wondering at what it sees
out of any face I turn to—
any dimmed, peeling face
laid before me on a table,

reproduced expertly on
a glossy, generous page.

AN OLD ROUTE

for William Crout

Beginning at sea,
you celebrate your birthday
seated at the Captain's
table, the very way

you had it all plotted out in a dream.
Later that night in bed
corks pop in your ears,
flashbulbs blossom on your eyelids.

Arriving in port,
you assess the bazaar at ease,
buying here a native wine,
here, an ebony bookend.

Dutifully the port people
learn to tell you from a distance,
riding the coast road
or supping under canopies.

Time comes to retire inland.
There the citied plain abruptly
juts into mountains.
Still below the snowline,

trees incline to be unburdened
of the fruits you never found in wagons.
Higher amid the rarefied
air, you unstrap unneeded weight.

From the bald summit, you see
after all the downgrade,
belted with believer's green,
but in the end, sand.

You notice that of all things
there is no end to that.
Sun flash and circling bird
signal you down.

Unfreighted when it comes
to inhabit deserts,
the mind reverts
to axioms:

*One
is alone
by definition;*

*skin burns, bone
bleaches
and it is
all one.*

IN THE ATTIC

Is this how Heaven is furnished? Kicked upstairs,
the stuff of many mansions under one roof.
Tables with knobby ankles, spindly chairs
nested like Chinese boxes, Chinese boxes;
an oval mirror coated with trackless dust
waiting to be profaned by a child's finger.
Five groaningly heavy cartons full
of fifty years of the *National Geographic*.
Nothing, it seems, is lost, only relocated.
The blanket chest is loaded with hoary trinkets:
a shaving mug from the St. Louis Exposition,
a Prayer Book great-uncle Cartwright carried to battle
in his breast pocket where it stopped a bullet.
A sliver of marble picked up once in Athens,
now labeled: "Adelaide. From the Parthenon."
All of these things wrapped up in soft clean rags,
I know without lifting the lid. The one end window,
tiny, triangular, intricate to open,
lets in a grainy light too weak to brave
the clutter of far corners. A bristling arm
of pine preempts whatever view there might be.
Outdoors, I know, the air is edged with autumn
but summer heat still harbors under these beams,
a hibernating warmth. Maybe that was why
as a child once, up here on a hunt after toys,
I fell asleep on a sheet-covered davenport.
The family searched for an hour before they found me.
Dinner was late that night. I peer about now,
so absently I almost bump with my nose
the most benign of spiders, dry-brown as a crumb
of tobacco, afloat on a single-strand ladder.
He waddles briskly up and out of sight
to his nest in a rafter's angle. Enough of this.
I came up after a winter coat. Uncoffined,
it hangs on my arm like something somebody shot,

a fair enough trophy. For the rest, let the spider
officiate, slight proprietor of the past.
For all we know the future is his also.

SNAKE CROSSING

Bullet headed, horsewhip tailed,
soundless, side-winding, nattily scaled,
it is a wonder anything fully solid
should flow so vividly quick through every part.
It swipes from thicket into opposing thicket.
Marking an end to one day's wanderlust,
I stand in the crossed path with joints made gelid,
hoping to slow my jumpiness of heart,
eyeing the faint, linked esses in the dust,
a sketchy hiss that I spell out in silence.

A MAN AND HIS WATCH

1.

Awake too early, even before false dawn,
he heard its tick from where he'd laid it down.
The webs of sleep still hung in bleary tatters;
he could see nothing in the room except
off to the left, at rest on edge, that dial
whose luminous darts endured their endless ambit.
The tick fell heavier than it did by day,
more adamant or more admonitory,
as if a dark spell might intensify
the burden of its rhythmless recital.
But there was only the absence of other sound
to thank for that. He recalled a warm afternoon
when after an hour of making love that seemed
perfect as flesh could hope to bestow or be blessed with
he lay back with his arm over his eyes
and heard it about its business on the bureau:
loud then too, though the room was filled with light.

2.

At 8:23 one morning it stopped dead.
Shaking it, rapping it on a table top
roused no reaction. It was almost indecently
self-conscious of an artifact, he thought,
to witness by its ultimate, mute expression
to the true moment of its own demise.
The hands, hung in a fixed and helpless V,
pointed apparently past their own tight compass
toward some far termini off the cosmic schedule.
He took it to a taciturn Swede whose fingers,
given a shift in superintending will,
could have made a career of cracking safes.
A spring and a bit of cleaning did the trick,
restored a world of order to his wrist,
the comfort of keeping tabs on wasted time.

3.

These were anomalies. Typically its behavior
has been to abide an unobtrusive servant.
An uncle, elderly, who'd never married,
died and left him a whole houseful of clocks.
All of them ran, and not a one kept pace
with any other. Two minutes each side of an hour
loosed a barrage of bongs and cuckoo-hoots.
It was like living with a German band.
He sold the lot, and bought himself the watch
herein referred to, wonderfully less abrasive
a token of mortality, he reasoned:
no up-to-the-minute news you didn't ask for.
And so it goes—or so they go together,
meeting appointments. Moving his arm he winds
this diligent disc, forgotten till consulted,
taking perpetual measure of the pulse
its platinum links luxuriously surround.
A half-handcuff. And only very lately
has he begun to feel its intimate weight.

II

BURNING ABORTIVE POEMS

Born to order, impromptu flame,
muttering revolt against
bulwarks of brick and screen;

bodiless polemic, punk,
poormouth, all aspiring tongue
and no abiding belly;

subjugated, starved consumer,
you will take what you are fed.
Here, spirit away in essence

to the indifferent heaven all
that isn't destined ash
in these unlucky efforts;

add to the reeling air my own
hesitant dab of oh, so
carefully distilled pollution.

Now I might say, Forgive me
for the mildly obscene
narrow whiff of sacrifice—

once these words seemed to me
to carry a cleaner smell . . . But who
is there for me to chatter to?

No late oblation then,
not to earth or sea
or overburdened sky; but

a purge pure and simple
for my benefit and that
of the hungering element.

Fire, already past your peak,
trembling to extinction on
a heap of black confetti—

you do your feeding credit due,
brief light and little heat.
Feaster never fasting,

you are what you eat.
And I, I am not
what I write. Not yet.

THE TASTE OF FAILURE

It strikes you as odd and out-of-the-way at first,
a sort of Middle Eastern salad dressing.

You try it on different areas of the tongue,
you can't quite place all the ingredients,

you tell yourself it isn't actually rancid,
it's just the way those have-not cultures like it.

It's cheap and it sort of grows on you.
Maybe you might want to order a second helping.

Funny the way the people at neighboring tables
lean over dishes you didn't see on the menu,

talking in rapt tones about "the Smell of Success."
The sensory metaphor differs in speaking of Failure,

perhaps because men cling grimly to positive concepts.
It does taste better than it smells.

SKIMMING A SURFACE

for I. A. Richards

Consider a moment the land of Euclidean figures, existing
back of all this sensible rubble and rut,
turbulent air and tar water, stump and fungus,
all too apparently real and finally too
corruptible to maintain the mind's allegiance.
Think, how behind all the natural accidents,
rimless, odorless, colorless planes unroll
to fabled infinity in whatever directions
are the most economical. Such a world has
points in its favor, it being restful to contemplate
order for once established above all challenge:
dust has never once been known to alight there,
no missing piece affronts the jigsaw puzzle, and
there *is* no imbecile puzzle, as every conceivable
option has been weighed and any conflict foreclosed.
Ought we then to apply for a rapid translation?
Drawbacks there may be, which we can only surmise.
One comes just now to mind. Let us select, for an
apt illustration, two orbs of equal dimension,
each one acceptable as an image of God; that is,
each one a perfect sphere. Now, were two such
bodies ever to touch, their meeting would needfully be
confined to one single point, then held in common.
Contact beyond this point means penetration,
identities experiencing double violation.
Which could indicate that in that ideal kingdom
it would ask fortitude to be oneself and yet keep
in touch, as one might care to, with neighboring relations.

AESOP IN OUR TIME

How entertained are we entitled to be, if the fox
        fumbles at getting his grapes?
You give a perennial malcontent enough knocks
and before you know it he up and rapes

somebody's prize lamb in a pasture somewhere
        or he goes after the goose
that lays eggs of a grade increasingly rare
and hard to find. One nutty fox on the loose

may not be reason enough to despair of the state
        of society; but when I read
that donkeys are dressing in lion hides of late,
or mastiffs preempting the mangers, I must concede

I am depressed with the general trend of fable.
        Too often the fascist ants
finish up smug behind their scavengers' table,
baiting an underfed grasshopper to dance.

Simple enough to project how the arts will fare
        under the winter regime:
fiddler's pay will be nibbled down to a bare
nutshell, with a proportionate fall in esteem.

And if I ever go sing on Establishment Street
        and the ants open their doors,
would I stoop to go in, perform and warm my feet?
You bet I would. The moral is all yours.

A LETTER FROM BEHIND THE LINES

Last week the giants took over the city,
trundled down out of the mountains and that was that.
They cordoned off blocks with telephone cable,
they stationed scouts on the waterways, two to a tug.
First they were nowhere, then they were everywhere,
tramping up and down and casting their massive shadows,
sending their blunt, disinterested glances
into fifth-storey windows. If you could have seen them,
seen up close their Alpine pallor, the eyes
icy and unamused, the carroty hair
tufting their bullety skulls and bludgeoning fists—
you would have found it easy to swallow your scruples,
turn and cooperate. Only a few
executions by summary mauling were needed to cow
the discerning public. Once having taken our measure,
they were not likely to sweat in their weighty sleep
for dreaming of us and our slingshots. Something
now of an orderly scene has returned to the fore,
scanty but regular rations of pickled meats
and powdered milk by now have persuaded some
to trust the invader's promises of prosperity,
plus universal love, justice, and hygiene.
Newspapers vie with each other in voicing approval.
Public confidence props us, yet
nobody ventures outside unnecessarily. Most
men are edgy; most women slightly insane. (Giants,
so we are told anyway, are demanding lovers.)
It's still difficult to sleep. You can hear them playing
tiddlywinks with manhole covers.

NOT ANSWERING LETTERS

The postmarks are unique and yet oddly anonymous,
smudgy fingermarks you would expect a child
to put on anything white. And postage stamps
paying heed to centennials soon lose currency.
I shudder to think of how my handwriting has changed
over all these years and will again, perhaps,
before I brace myself to retrieve the reins
of my runaway correspondence rearing ahead of me.
Even not opening letters would have to be better
than letting them fester like this: the longer they lie
knifed open, the higher the edgy heap,
the more they come to remind you of husbandless women
bulking at the far end of the lunch counter,
draped in filmy gray raincoats. They lift their chins
to look at you a long moment, so that you know
it is for your sake that the egg salad sandwich
lies on the plate neglected. You feel like saying,
But what can I do? So too with these,
once innocent friendly notes now steadily turning
to pages of accusation. The fault is my own.
And yet if I ever answered most of these letters
the best I could manage to say would hardly be any
better than notes I carefully penned at age seven
to relatives who required them, saying
HELLO. I AM FINE. I HOPE YOU ARE THE SAME.

TO JAMES ATLAS

On His Way to Brazil

Rummaging now through a book whose generic name
is the same as yours, Miss Bishop's line recurs to me:
"More delicate than the historians' are the map-makers' colors."
Brazil, of course, would bring that lady to mind.
In this particular version Brazil is pink-orange,
and, the page being glossy, exhibits the sheen
of a shell, the kind that crimps and curves like an ear
and imitates the ocean to the idle ears of men.
One may trace the Amazon as one might follow
the life line along the palm of a gigantic hand,
or notice again in contemplating the coast
the hauteur in which the uplifted nose
of the nation disdains the suppliant sea.
Cities appear to be coastal or threaded
together by rivers, names look almost pronounceable;
on its face it presents a rather agreeable profile;
(although one reads it can take ten years or more
to install a telephone, barring bribes, in Rio).

Judging from what we have read in *Questions of Travel*
Brazil, if you open your eyes to it, ought to afford you
no end of exotic copy; so I shall wait for your poems.
Meanwhile, if I myself am to be like Burton,
traveling "but in map or card,"
let me select for my own map one
endearingly approximate,
perhaps an archaic New World map
with whole peninsulas grandly ignored,
with miracle-tressed, exuberant winds
trumpeting from the four gilded corners,
puckering lips, ballooning cheeks, perpetually deflating.
Galleons tidily rigged and spuming
whales may here and there interrupt the waves;

every location must be denoted in Latin.
For that I shall need a volume a little less current.
For yourself, James, bon voyage; enjoy yourself, do
your traveling, and, as far as you can, mine too.

THE FIRST DAY OF SPRING

Not rain really. Sprigs of mist
busy amid a whitish sky.
I keep to my regimen. You can find me
bookish as ever, bent to arcane
disciplines, bristling indices,
commentaries on commentaries,
any excuse for treating
text as fertile pretext.

Grown intent I darken
defenseless margins with my
cabalistic doodles,

forking twigs fret against
the glass, weeks away
from leafing, like wishbones
hung up for luck.

Wisdom is long in coming.
Don't you be.

MID-JULY

After a dozen rainless days
a single walk across the vacant lot
will spoil a shoeshine; clumps of blistered grass
droop dulled from tip to root with dust.
Along the borders random shreds of glass
smack the eye with amber glare at noon.
It is enough to send one soon
indoors, to find that other surfaces
are bent on misbehaving: shirts cling
determinedly to shoulder blades,
varnished chair arms won't let go of elbows.

To sit and contemplate the sagging, moist
centerfold of the year
wonderfully magnifies one's grievances.
It is one of those scientific laws:
an urge for tabulating minor flaws
increases with the temperature.
I prove it by experiment each day.
But still, a poorly patched kitchen screen,
salt clotting the shaker holes,
a half cucumber going bad,
even the fact of tomorrow's being my birthday,

these, while they feed my suspicion that I have been had,
I feel I might put up with, even keep
a demeanor more nearly approaching grace
if I didn't have to watch for a long minute
(without a wink, immobilized by heat)
among the crumbs left from lunch
a housefly cleansing delicately her face.

SMALL HOURS

Lights out: a room
and a half away, the kitchen
faucet comes alive
without human prompting;
it must be in league
with the glum refrigerator
that hums something modern
and severe to itself
ten minutes at a time
till it stops with a clunk.

Once begun, the trickle
irks without mercy;
oriental torture
by remote control.
Irregular enough
to keep us awake,
not enough irregular
to keep us entertained.

It's without sparkle
and uncollected—
not like the icicle's
noonday tear,
not like the lucid
upended bells
of fluid that beam
from the dinner crystal.

It hasn't induced us
to waterfall dreams;
didactic drop
upon drop develop
a too-familiar tale
of radical repairs
that somehow don't

ever happen to be done
during the time
they dirge away damply.

So, what to do?
Take a wrench to it?
Not us; impossible.
Score it to a tune,
have it do *Singing in the Rain.*
Think: it is endless
but it is all ending.
Plip, plop, *ad*
infinitum, drip or drop . . .
It all goes down the drain.

MORNING MESSAGE

Your breathing, deep or drifting into shallow,
came to me as I tossed from ear to ear
all night awake, wishing that I might follow
along the untroubled passage I could hear

slumber affording you—a generous current,
rinsing the day's detritus from the brain.
Simple, if you had been there, but you weren't.
You were a hundred miles away in Maine.

I knew your innocent ease at shunting care:
that you were then asleep was a sound wager.
But that your breath should float to me from there
would stagger the least serious physics major.

Is there an ether of attracted souls
to kite their stirrings over unhappy gaps?
Or do our minds, like magnets, reverse poles
in a rich trade of dreams? A dim "perhaps"

is all that morning finds me in a mood
to answer, now a meddling light has crept
about me to lay bare my solitude,
and no one now inquires how I slept.

Love or a midnight twisting of the nerves
brought me this quickened hearing of the blind
that nobody with two working eyes deserves.
I wonder, could your night have been as kind?

RENOVATIONS

A twist, a little fiddling
with temperature, then in:
and each day the unstinting
downrush of liquid lines
sprung from a silvery nozzle
will move a mind half drowsing
to misty appreciations.

Remarkable how a mere eight
hours between sheets, followed
by eight minutes under a gentle
cataract can return to view
a rinsed original
whose rested limbs hang gladly,
clothed in a grace of steam,
whose most unruly member droops
at ease in the hot douse.

To look down and decide again
that dinginess isn't endemic,
to notice again that this
tough-to-waken lanky mass
of carnal accidents
will come clean with a few scrubs
as many days as need be,

can generate sufficient pure
euphoria to bedew
each white, receptive tile
walling round the curtained rite.

When the last trails of lather
have slid away and the flow
of the fountain again is sealed,
a hovering wonder lingers
long enough to allow me
to wipe the flat fog away

from the medicine chest mirror,
and look full on the face I know
better and less than others.
And he looks back . . .

And I get in my "Good morning"
before his own habitual
"So now, get a move on"—which
I do, still a bit damp.

LOOKING OUT

The neighbor's kid has fallen out of his wagon
and skinned his knees, hands and chin on the sidewalk.
Lucky if he managed to keep his teeth,
I think, looking around you while you talk,

out the window, waiting to see his mother
come, as she will, not soon enough, but soon.
She will lift him up from the bloody, punishing earth
and soften his racket with a consoling croon.

Until she comes he brandishes his stigmata
and bellows his accusations at the sky.
My window's shut. Is hers? Until she comes,
you have my ear, his cries have caught my eye.

Breakfast is no time to have to make decisions
and there is the kid howling out at the curb.
Looking deliberately past your cooling eggs, your chill face,
I wish there were more to this order I might disturb,

that goodness would sugar this concrete world of ours,
putting to rights things done and left undone,
or even that simple hurts could steal our attention
from this or that more complicated one.

SIMILE

Like a drunk after a knock-down, drag-out night,
steering a weird course through a city square
on the point of dawn with no other soul in sight
save pigeons, whom he orders into the air,
whose iridescent throats in rising light
assuage his thirst for purple—uncontrite,
a poet wanders prey to his own mad dare,
wobbles amid words, startles them into flight.

III

SAFE ON FRIENDLY SOIL

for Peter and Alex Theroux

Bells, and more bells batter the April air;
even deep within walls they reach our ears.
Ending the Paschal Liturgy, our Patriarch
falters his final blessing. Tears invade
my eyes so that I scarcely see the household
bowing me down the aisle. By the stoup
Marta and Josef, touchingly well-attired,
present me, on behalf of all the servants,
a dozen eggs, stenciled in wax and lacquered.
The very sort that coveys of convent children,
smocked in white and dropping speechless curtseys,
handed us every Easter. What of those
we once might hand each other?—filigreed fantasies,
hinging in half to furnish snuff or powder,
or portraits of ourselves on ivory.
One of them grandly hatched a jeweled bird,
crafted to flap his wings and twang a waltz.
Nested in neutral vaults now, or as need
arises, changed for unfantastic cash.
Infrequent, those necessities, while yet
my royal brother-in-law is pleased to lend
a floor of his Winter Palace to my court.
I pass a vague salute to those who linger
about the chapel door, and stride upstairs,
impatient to have off these epaulets,
to lift from my neck by its blue and silver loop
the Order of St. Boris and St. Gleb—
a ponderous cross for mortal flesh to bear.
Dismantling my regalia, I can stare
out of my casement on a far-receding

range of respectable blocks of brick and stucco,
untopped by tiled domes or rainbow roofs—
my capital's antiquated stratagems
to court the shyest rays of the northern sun.

Our present milieu deprecates display;
this tunic, stuck with clusterings of braid,
hangs fitlier in a press than on one's back,
and leveling urges undermine the soul.
Writing my memoirs to remind myself
of who I was, I drop the royal We.
My audiences, or rather, interviews
with friendly journalists wax democratic.
I lose some dignity by nattering on
at tedious length about my other losses,
indulging in the luxury of complaint
as an abused, untitled subject might.
To speak at large invites absurdities,
encourages men to calculate my loss
in common terms and low comparisons:
a fickle mistress, an estate foreclosed,
a heifer hit by a train, a cigarette case
dropped at the Opera, missed at intermission,
advertised for in Personals, never found.
Democracy is not the worst of dooms,
but a life no analogies can circle
borders on being not a life at all.

Yet others have proved less equipped than I
to cope with our descent to sober coats.
Our toppling's cursed my unadaptive Queen
with an abiding lack of equilibrium.
She speaks but little, lives behind drawn blinds,
passing her hours cloistered with canaries.
Their cage fills half a room, their twitters echo
along crepuscular corridors like the sighs
of souls in Limbo.
                                    Thus am I reduced

to search for human intercourse in servants,
or meetings with my Cabinet, which consists
of no one now but Kryptov. On he mutters,
spreading out maps and telegrams in cipher,
champing his barely endurable black cigarettes,
in all too many ways my Minister
Without Portfolio. He abounds in hope.
"They can't last six more months," he reassures me,
without fail, twice a year. I nod and smile,
and wave him off to his émigré café
where messages of dire import are passed
between his cup and saucer. After that
he goes to God knows where—the address alters
every few weeks: he fears assassination.
A touch vainglorious, some would say, in that.

My own intrigues are inwardly directed.
They are designed to keep within close bounds
moods of misanthropy and vain regret.
What happened, happened. Blood patching the snow,
boxcars overturned and burning, horses
thrown to the ground in shuddering squeals of pain—
all that belongs to chaos breaking in;
it has no bearing on an afternoon
soon to be wasted pacing the Embankment
blurred with river mist and loud with tongues
deemed less obscure than mine. The echoing barter
bemuses me till I turn back at dusk.
When streetlamps, wanly haloed, wetly shine,
a quieter memory of our casting out
gathers and glides in underneath my guard:
As our unmarked train rumbled over the border,
I craned my neck for a final look and saw
a band of peasants moving down a field,
quick to cock hay under a threat of rain.
They kept pace with each other, a drab phalanx,
rhythmic in every stab and cumbrous lift.

Under that sky their forks gave off no glimmer.
They might have posed for Millet, made for their work,
oblivious of the personage passing by them,
passing from them under a plume of steam.
The rushing air, gritty and cold, bestowed me
an initial, numbing taste of anonymity
which this day's walk should serve to reconfirm.

If ever I get to it, freed of tin and tinsel.
Ribbons and tassels masquerade the bed;
I shoulder a plain topcoat while overhead
morning is counted out; the choir of bells
come to rest one by one until a single
note is all that's left, announcing noon.
Twelve, and a pause extends to point an ending.
The last vibrations spent, the massive shells
hang plumb and clumsy. Lacking the proof of music,
they might as well be so much toneless lead.
Strict masochists, they only sing when struck,
or sing a different tune when melted down
and cast anew as cannon. That, too, happened.
But we forget ourselves. We'd best be off,
and walk awhile and meet the wonted image.
The pitchfork men. I wish I'd known them better.

IV

BIRTH OF A CRITICAL SPIRIT

for Michael Johnston

Ten years old, on his annual summer visit,
he noticed how much easier, on the whole,
it was to be grandson, nephew—not a son.
Uncle and Aunt, married as much to the farm
as to each other, left him alone. Grandfather
napped in the parlor under a newspaper tent.
Grandmother kept to the kitchen, busy with dough.
He didn't feel unwanted, only free.
He ran in the far pasture dodging cowflops
and mildly annoying cows, or fished for minnows.
Mostly he sat against the springhouse wall,
its boards black with damp and cool to his back,
reading his books on lower forms of life.

A memorable summer: some weeks before,
he had been fitted for his first eyeglasses.
Types of fodder, once all a wash of green,
now took bows, here timothy, there alfalfa.
Print lay flat on the page, its glimmer gone.
He read unmindful of time, and came to supper
each night equipped with queasy natural facts:
the flatworm's way of growing back a head
no matter how many times you cut it off;
the flounder's migrating eyes; the lady scorpion
capping a tryst by gobbling up her mate.
The seagull's regurgitant feeding of its chicks . . .
"Please, not at the table." That was his aunt.
His uncle, though, would hasten to mend matters:
"That's all right, tell us more about the scorpions."
Grandfather grinned, or came as close to grinning

as a midwestern patriarch might. Grandmother
managed a quick retreat by stacking plates
and soon from the kitchen a soapy clatter arose.

Was it that night it occurred to him that *they*
were in the way of being specimens?—
Aunt, dabbing a napkin at an upper
lip that never needed such attentions,
Uncle, tilting back in a creaky chair,
lacing satisfied thumbs in frayed suspenders.
How do you put a finger on such a moment?
Enough to say, sitting there, one summer evening,
hearing the buzz and thud behind his back
of June bugs stupidly battering the screen,
rubbing a darned spot on the table cloth
as if he were a beginner reading Braille,
he swore himself to singularity,
detachment, living in the light of science.
His insights would be his, not other men's.
Looking up, he saw his people stirring
their coffee, smiling at him through the lens.

THE POEM

This is a restless stone without a sweater.
This is a place where lightning landed twice.
This is a fractured camel's delicate burden.
This is the knowing marrow of the bones.

This is a pot assailing a kindred kettle.
This is the one bad apple in the bin.
This is the salt that went outside for savor.
This is the silence that you ache to mend.

This is the latest bridge that was burnt behind you.
This is the spilled milk that swallows tears.
This is a bitten hand still dealing meat out.
This is a paper bag containing your rage.

This is the scratch you start from.
This is a hound's tooth grinding itself clean.
This is the life! This is the road not taken.
This is a cat in love with the number nine.

This is an elephant learning to be forgetful.
This is a spade identified as such.
This is a house divided and still standing.
This is the ground you walk on answering prayers.

A LIVING

Our milkman in midwinter must
begin his round by dark,
or marginal light, when only size
marks off a barn from a house.
All to himself a rising road,
he must have memorized by now
the pallid, high-peaked gables
grinning against the hills like fossil teeth.

On mornings that cut
between glove and cuff,
when frost whitens further the wan grass,
he lurches up our corrugated drive—
heard and not seen, in lieu of a rooster.
Full bottles clank, empties tinkle
like a child's carillon.
And how does he like his life?

At Christmastime we leave him
five dollars in an envelope.
He signs his thank-you note,
"Your Milkman." It allows us
to fancy him as keen about his work,
and that in a way we're never apt to be.

Which is or is not a blessing. Soon
his grating brake lets go
and he bumps his puttering truck
away in the pink distance
whose glow has barely touched our eastern panes.
Sympathy follows only so far,
then settles back to bed-level,
decrees we find one another
anew by the first light of day
and while we have it, husband close
our meager, soon-to-escape-us hoard of warmth.

IN WITNESS

for Robert Fitzgerald

My way lay through a wood.
Under a guise of trees
all my old familiars stood,
off limits by law.
I recognized the species
of every one I saw,

even despite the lack
of leaves on all that lumber.
Now that I was back
I dropped my old esteem
and sought amid their number
a remnant to redeem.

I snapped a twig or two
to make a test,
and saw the blood flow
from the wormy bark.
I wandered west,
trailed after by the dark.

Gathering branches here and there
I could dream that I was led
by the Harrower
of the waste, wild land
who went harvesting the dead
with no hook but a hand.

One twig was sound and green—
that one I would keep.
I came to a clearing then,
round, empty and as good
as any place to sleep.
There I dumped my dead wood

and kindled it to fire
the better to banish fear.
But as the flame grew higher
my single green twig cried,
"Lord, if you had been here
my brothers had not died."

RECESSIONAL

And we, too, have witnessed
empire put downhill.
Bristling in our own backyard,
vegetable tribes resist
the niceties of our will—
what the settling men found hard
to settle is hard still.

Seed released outruns the sower,
taking sway over the land;
tussock and the twig impede
the progress of the mower.
Beds we civilized by hand
reinstate the exiled weed,
soil behaves like sand.

Primal imps of the perverse
are garden gods, infusing vices
into the veins of all we grow.
Ripening melons turn for the worse,
set on never becoming slices.
Every willfully ailing row
puts me in mind of winter prices.

And it puts me in mind of Cain,
feeling murderous in the field.
How could his or any garden
hope to avoid the Lord's disdain
in view of Eden's yield?
Cain wore his mark of pardon
even after his forehead healed;

and the heirs to his estate
differ intensely over its worth,
but they live the lives they earn.
Labor is their enduring trait,
bringing the proud towns to birth

that we abandon in our turn
to labor in the earth.

THERE

There where the lion dines on straw
and walks at ease with dogs and men,
and a boy's idling fingers draw
the unfanged adder out of his den;

and the hills lift up leafy hands,
lemon, cedar, and olive scented,
blessing the herbed and honeyed lands
where the twelve tribes at last are tented;

there where the river bangled with amber
journeys to fields made full of grain,
and the men rafted over remember
not one moment of wilderness pain;

and the dove mounts her woven house
high in the teeming Tree of Life,
fruit of whose glancing, tropic boughs
drops to the hand without a knife:

Lord of the poor, who roared from Zion,
sounding the way of David's heir,
there where the lamb is Judah's lion,
there is our home. Then lead us there.

THE PAUSE

Only a slow-growing forest, met with
in the warming cleft of summer,
would have hosted such a moment—
that is where we were.

No living owner's name
was posted where we came to earth.
Slivered seed-hulls, winter litter,
lay round like brown manna,

in the oval clearing abandoned
cones dried and raveled to tinder.
Nearby a forking stream
swam over tracts of pebbles, they

were creviced and gray as pebbles
dug from the dark side of the moon.
How shall I say what happened?
Summer came to a standstill,

birds grew sober, limp air mingled
into the crowns of trees and put away
puffing, maybe for good.
The stream ran sudden as blood

but it was all that ran.
Even our fates stood off awhile,
tireless, but disengaged,
broadly considering us the way

we might look at children tranced in play.
Cool eyes fanned over us, like leaf-shadows.
Halfway up the pines sunlight
may have played, for all I know,

in needles, priming the points—but
by then our eyes were shut.

HEAT WAVE

That power-sapping fan that hacks the air,
sending the tepid slices of it flying,
lacks power and aim alike to land them where
you and I inconveniently are lying,

all of a midnight on the third day straight
of stifling in our inner-city furnace—
as if the town, reflecting urban hate,
had mustered all its surfaces to burn us.

The neighbor's radio whines out wise advice,
dictating to the audience it serves:
Lights out and lemonade and lots of ice.
Diminish bodily contact. Save your nerves.

But temperate counsels such as these are lost
on you and me who meet to mingle sweat,
clinging as though to foil invading frost.
Tonight our native heats are happily met;

tonight considerations pitched beyond
comfort endure, and, having drawn together
the pair of us in such a godly bond,
stand fair to weather out ungodly weather.

CLIMB AND CLOUDBURST

The rain held off until
the cabin came in sight,
capping the ragged hill,
at home upon its height.

Just then, the grumbling dyke
above it sharply cracked
and the object of our hike
was cloaked in cataract.

Quickstep and steepening trail
soon led us to the door
and water by the pail
rolled off us on the floor.

You scouted round for kindling.
Through a split pane of glass
I saw the downpour dwindling,
allowing sun to pass

amid the prisming threads
that graced a row of trees,
affording credulous heads
a glimpse of light and ease;

not a mere dark and damp
disorder out of doors
against which men encamp,
toting unsettled scores.

A pattern: I could trace
the drift of each thin drop
to its appointed place....
When it all ticked to a stop,

it crossed my mind that we'd
be better for this rinsing,
but not my lips—you'd need
some serious convincing.

*What an unholy botch
this is!* So you might feel.
I turned around to watch
the papery shavings peel

beneath your practiced knife
for us to put a light to,
and felt better about my life
than I had any right to.

PRACTICE

It wasn't anything special: my quick-handed cousin
    managed to grab a snake out of the pasture
edging my uncle's stream; he whipped it hard
    against a nearby boulder, hung it stunned
over a low tree limb, and took his practice.

    The hollow pop of the BB rifle couldn't
have traveled far at all, and yet to me
    it sounded loud. I looked down at the water
brown as beer, busy with silt, unevenly
    running over the flat rocks—some of those,
I knew, could show the feathery prints of shells.

    Patches of cress, a queer fluorescent green,
swayed in the quiet current. The pop again,
    answered every time by a trifling tap
as pellet after pellet peckered the bark.

    I looked and saw the sun glisten off the black
upside-down U (how, I can never remember,
    is the lucky way to hang up a horseshoe?)—it wasn't
moving much, his aim was off that afternoon.

    It wasn't anything special, and yet I swear
it taught me something of what the flesh is heir to;
    my own skin crawled, I said, I say, sweet instinct,
quailing terror of guts, prevent my hands
    from visiting the inflictions they may itch to
upon the dumb and hapless happening past.

GRASS WIDOWS

Your dandelions dotting half
a casual summer lawn
mature to let their fertile chaff
uncouple and be gone;

a chance breeze or a child's puff
yellow-buttons leagues of green.
Call it a Life Force? Call it fluff.
The tatty clusters mean

whatever you may wish them to,
breathing abroad the seed
that's found a go-between in you.
Insouciantly weed,

these have neither toiled nor spun:
like their lily neighbor
lean at ease in rain and sun,
blest for lack of labor.

And labor's lost. Grass goes unmown.
You watch them grow up gold
and thick as midnight stars were shown
to Abraham who was old.

ON BECOMING AN ALTAR BOY

Anno Aetatis XXVI

My dexterous, dear, demanding Lord,
what could have cozened You to press
these limbs, that know but loose accord,
with disciplines of fancy dress?

Vagrant attention slouching off,
omitted bows or hasty dips,
an incense-aggravated cough,
a myriad odd, nearsighted slips,

a double complement of thumbs,
terror of tripping on the stair—
pardon, if each poor mess becomes
the rueful pretext of a prayer.

Hands that deftly enough have gripped
the gimcrack men are daily sold
grow soundly ill-at-ease, equipped
with the best gifts a man could hold.

Yet blunders made in truth, in taste,
in trust, committed to the Cup,
incredibly escaping waste,
turn lustrous in their offering up.

So every week an hour or less
shows me a hope that, after all,
a Grace engaging clumsiness
will lift what trembling hands let fall.

MUSEUM COINS

Money must once have seemed
innocent, original,
a miracle mined and minted.
Men thought (some thought)
that gold ripened underground,
responding to a generous, piercing
influence of the sun.

No numismatist myself,
the shimmer of these enticed me
to blink over their display case,
conning the profiles that so
commandingly adorn their discs.
A score of our stodgy Miss
Liberties have tried
and failed to emulate them:
Athena, Alexander,
helmed gods and men,
heroic heads the race
in its youth relied on.

But what, I wonder, put it
into my head to wonder
which of the little, dimmer ones
was the obolus, the smaller-
than-bite-sized coin the bereaved
put under the tongue of a corpse
to pay the Ferryman?
Failure to pay meant a hundred years'
walk in the thorny woods.

Later, alone on a cool
marble bench in the lobby,
I held a dime to my lips
and tasted nothing more than a faint
flavor of use and abuse.
Children, of course, are always

swallowing coins, which seems less
silly somehow than tasting them.
I took my dime out of my mouth
and myself out of that museum,
onto a street where the August sun
poured forth an argosy.

To be born, to be brought up on earth
is so untold a good fortune,
it is like found money,
stumbled on every day.
What we conceive as our last
destination is our own business.
Let each man look to his own,
I say to quiet my heart
that would have me blurting out
what few of my friends believe:
*We go where Love would have us go,
the ferrying there is free.*

OLD PHOTOGRAPH

No man, they say, is a hero to his valet.
Since I have always served as my own valet
self-adulation rarely has overwhelmed me.
I can be decently cool, confronted with this,
but can't deny an interest. Look at this fellow,
posed in a college courtyard, very improbably
vacant but for him. No beard as yet,
but an unkempt mustache, and an excessive
amount of chin that covering up wouldn't hurt.
The head tilts to the left, and the left eyebrow
is arched with an air benignly quizzical.
The left eye underneath displays the amazing
peripheral vision that kept him out of the army.
A few zits; razor rash. But less predictably,
the lips bend up in a bland, unworried curve.
Could life behind that brick-and-ivy backdrop
truly have left him so little traumatized?
It could be acting, awkwardness for a moment
contained by force of will. Or it could be
a fact of history: maybe those days and nights
heavy with insubstantial gropings weren't,
after all, utter hell. (If anyone *died*
of embarrassment, who would live past adolescence?)
In any case, that confident smile now
can only strike dismay in the beholder
who knows how many corners blithely cut
in those days needed years of rounding off.
A proud ass or a poor bastard—take your pick.
Now back, and living a block away from where
a roommate, on a periodic binge
of wasting film, preserved for future reference
this portrait of The Poet Under Twenty,
I shake my head in reminiscent judgment:
All he was good at, now and then, was writing.
A bit severe? A bit too baldly stated. . . .

I wouldn't trust him, then or now or ever,
with anything more serious than words, ·
but feel he meant well, as I hope I do.

ANOTHER DAY

That morning tide, that upswing of the air,
wages against the wing of the house I lie in;
tuning now to its waves, my curtain rings
clink like a bustling housekeeper's bunch of keys.
Sleepers, awake: for doors and stairs are creaking musically,
skirling as though the entire house
were stretching in the sun,
letting the dew steam off its chalky shingles.
Linen quivers; a warm, barny smell
rides in at the window. Light is taking sway:

the firmament of shadow overhead
sifts out of the room, revealing
unmysterious ceiling. Square and white,
its four corners boast no dangling spies.
Once again I dreamt of dead relations,
Grandmother in the garden, another summer,
pinching a done flower from its stem,
yesterday's day-lily.
Handing it to me absently, passing on
—into what hidden place? No protocol
governs these wordless meetings.

So often now I'm strange to my own skin.
I could be standing there at the door—
not now, but twenty years from now—
taking this in, from the sun's first
foothold, a thin, quaking beam
where pinhead seraphs conjured out of dust
exult and swarm. And see, my heavier
self lies long and motionless in bed,
grown a sounder sleeper, guessing nothing at all,
till the light widens, and the wind
blows the white curtains in.